The Apple Tree

The Apple Tree

POEMS

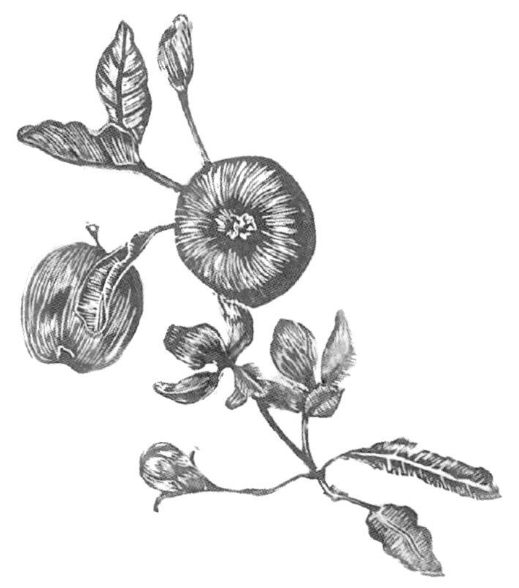

Catherine Arnold

Bauhan Publishing
PETERBOROUGH NEW HAMPSHIRE
2025

ISBN: 978-087233-388-8
Library of Congress Cataloging-in-Publication Data

Names: Arnold, Catherine, 1967- author.
Title: The apple tree : poems / Catherine Arnold.
Other titles: Apple tree (Compilation)
Description: Peterborough, New Hampshire : Bauhan Publishing, 2025. |
Identifiers: LCCN 2025003876 (print) | LCCN 2025003877 (ebook) | ISBN 9780872333888 (paperback) | ISBN 9780872333895 (ebook)
Subjects: LCGFT: Poetry.
Classification: LCC PS3601.R58266 A85 2025 (print) | LCC PS3601.R58266 (ebook) | DDC 811/.6--dc23/eng/20250207
LC record available at https://lccn.loc.gov/2025003876
LC ebook record available at https://lccn.loc.gov/2025003877

Book design by Sarah Bauhan;
Cover design by Henry James
Printed by Versa Press
Cover image: "King Parrots in the Apple Tree"
by Marion Lynk. www.marionlynk.com, used by permission

To reach Catherine: www.catherinearnold.com

PO BOX 117 PETERBOROUGH NEW HAMPSHIRE 03458
603-567-4430
WWW.BAUHANPUBLISHING.COM

MANUFACTURED IN THE UNITED STATES OF AMERICA

To my two beloveds,
Victor and Stella

CONTENTS

PART ONE: PERISHABLE

The Apple Tree 11
His Hands 16
The Raffle 18
Earrings 20
The Button Collector 21
The House 22
In the Greenhouse 23
At the Inn 24
Tulips Require Partial Shade 26

PART TWO: AWE

Where Does the Rapunzel Go? 30
There Is No Formula for Fox 31
Love Poem: Daughter 32
Walking on a Keyboard 34
Planting 35
Two Figures on the Path 37
No Wonder 39
Wonder 40
A Child 41
The Mouse and the Hawk 42
Hurt 44
Elijah 45
A Demonstration 48
Life Jacket 49

PART THREE: THE SMALL DOMESTICS

Little Gratitudes 52
At the Salon 54
Butter and Milk and Sugar 56
The Only Unextraordinary Things 57
At This Distance Safely Brilliant 58
Thank You for Your Patience 59
Longing 60
Feasts 61
The Last Meal 62

PART FOUR: ANXIETIES

On the Clock 64
Hush 65
Small Word 66
Shatterproof 67
H Is Drawing 69

PART FIVE: THE SLEEPLESS EYE

Trapped 72
Witch 75
A Single Sleepless Eye 77
The Drummer 78
Each Small Castle Window 80
Bears 81
Acknowledgments 84

PART ONE

PERISHABLE

The Apple Tree

I

What do I remember
growing   in the house of apples?
Thirteen trees   cider every year
the fruit waiting   in the whitewashed shed   on pallets
cooling their flesh
(we don't talk about anything personal)
withering   waiting my turn   to go   under
the screws of the press
juice   pouring   into vats
to be drunk   to be swallowed   in hope   of intoxication
crushing the sweetness out.

Sitting in the tree   arms around the trunk
relying on the grain and pressure of the bark
to keep me steady
crying   when all tears are forbidden   not a graceful tear or two   No
weeping   disgusting   epic
tears falling into a silver bowl   held by a Grimm fairy.

Pain skewering the length of me
twisting out the core   as
I contemplate a second Fall
for the sin of a lie   that wasn't mine
my shins scraping   the crooked tree
staring at the grassy floor
knowing I cannot return   to the time before
knowing   I will not be forgiven
anticipating   the laws of exile
learning to do with scant
learning not to demand   repayment.

No more faith
No more grace   learning to live without
learning to push away.

II

Spinning the wound   into the thread   of my spine
watching the world move away
hiding   safe   except   for the trembling shake
when the wind comes through.

Waiting
watching my fingers harden into twigs
waiting   while the grim one holds the bowl   filling it up
(*Don't exaggerate*   they say
Don't make mountains...)
I paddle   through
the dirt   with my dim eyes
inviting darkness   holding it in
seeking the safety of small
earth-lined spaces
resting my knotted hands against the trunk
hoping your weight will guide me
knowing there is no forgiveness   (judgment holding steady)
knowing I will run away
oceans waiting
learning to grow   up.

III

I'm twenty   when I see it
Bernini's *Apollo and Daphne*
I recognize   the woman-girl

I am her averted face.

The instructor tells me it's about terror
but I see shelter in the bark
in the fast leafy spiral
I see a girl turning from the marble from that polished cold—
tensed ankles tight breath—
escaping into confidential green
into the lush ragged careless:
leaves shade apple tree.

I'd run
out of the stricken hard refined I want that transformation
I'd run
out of the stone block into flying leaves I'd take that
the swooping warm catch.

The instructor says the sculpture is about fear
I see liberation.

Into stone the sculptor cuts
the chisel makes the sinews (and I know
the cuts of the artist go all the way through:
the chisel makes the girl).

Daphne flees across the land
she's hiding running cut (*Don't exaggerate*)
Daphne I know you
Daphne your lips are sealed
running running apple-laurel
bristling child can you get there fast enough?

IV

What did I call you my girl
when you were stirring treading amniotic?
Sprout bud petal
and in time I watched you losing—
losing the ability to speak—your words disappearing
a few lost every week so that I learned to measure time backwards
words streaming backwards
to the point of their erasure
until the hush settled
until my mind became an echo chamber.
Each year the echo of your voice grew fainter
though your visionary lips kept moving ushering me back
to a time that could never
have existed.

I took your pulse through fever nights
nights that stretched but did not break
in the morning when I touched my skin
I found I'd petrified I'd turned to stone.

Ten years the silence ruled—
that was our sentence—
for ten years I was running
my mind exercising miracles
while you paced your unsharable thoughts.
Ten years and then you found another way
moving your fingers across the keys

one key   one letter   at a time
A-P-P-L-E   T-R-E-E
this tablet is alight   this wax is soft enough   to catch
and reveal   your intention.

I want to give you   an amulet
daughter   to protect you
a striped stone around your neck
a tiger's eye
Do not rest   Do not be captured
Do not agree to surrender.

Apollo and Daphne, sculpture by Gian Lorenzo Bernini, circa 1625.

His Hands

The warm brown feel of his hand   in mine
a link   I would have soldered to the chain
and tightened   if I could
so that his fingers wouldn't split   or break
the grip.

Walking in the blessing   of his hand   along
the edge of the canal   beside the amber-windowed houseboats
longing to be admitted   to the social light
then the sudden break   unanchoring
leaving   my palm opening and closing
gaping   like a fish's mouth.

Home: at the door   feet on the scraper
wellies off   and back
to the slow lugging of quiet   the punctured look
the longing
that learned to keep its counsel
preserving each walk between heavy sheets
of paper
a replica to admire   on hungry   days
a fern from this walk
a dandelion from that   screwing them down
between the creamy sheets
and waiting for the sap to drain.

A miraculous device   the flower press
placing a celandine   a forget-me-not   a nettle
between pillowy paper
strong enough to bear the memory
hoping that when   I rise from my chair

I'll discover myself pretty   a pretty one
who doesn't need to discipline
herself out of
desiring unnecessary things.

The Raffle

I

You can wear these   she said
the door closed   her footsteps retreated down the stairs
I was ten years old   sitting on the edge of the bed
looking at the   forked outlandish proposition
two stems joined   two frail   hollow   legs
for parceling muscle and skin   meting out   the silky fabric
the sensation of arriving   at implausible sophistication.

Lowering my foot into the net   watching it stretch
to cover my toes   vanishing   the nails
on the ends of my claws   turning them to sleek
because   you need to cover your claws
pull on the pretty hoof   become a mare   forget the wolf.

This fine   strained layer
this new skin   how I loved it
the woman's net and smother.

Sitting on the edge of the bed
I looked forward   to the party
we would play   *Musical Statues*   *Pass the Parcel*   *Tail on the Donkey*
and   other obsolete Victorian games
we would eat Jell-O shivering   in glass bowls
I would look for my own shape   scanning
the dimensions of the mold
eyeing the tracks I'd make   with my silken hooves
up and down the lonely   unpopulated   hills.

II

From *stockings*   Mum's old-fashioned word   I moved
to the land of *panty hose*   (absurd).

I was twenty   studying the score
the number   of denier   printed on the packet
calculating how much   of my skin's light   to cover
(the sprouting hair   the scales   all traces of the mammal)
traveling back   ten years old again   rising from the bed
preparing for the party
stepping   into new shoes   cork-heeled   simmering
so I'm strapped in
treading down my sole   (does the shoe fit   Cinderella?
let the sisters take out their knives
prepare   to chop off their toes).

Sitting on the edge of the bed
feeling the ripple slide down my spine
promising   knowledge   looming it into my skin
the humming veil   the pleasure of learning   to snare and offer
my legs.

Pass the parcel   sit down
for the raffle.

Earrings

I wore amber earrings   huge
they dragged me   pulled my ears down   like gravestones
and in each   was an incarcerated baby
showily dispensing tears
(which were unforgivable
I heard my mother's voice say
Get up   be a brave soldier)
but they did not   these infants
they went on weeping   keening.

The tears fell from the soles   of their trapped feet
like those old dolls that piss
I lifted my hands to touch   the tombstone earrings
and my fingers came away wet
I found   holes drilled into the stone
they cried   these infants   wept
I was affronted   by the crude display
So tasteless   said another voice   from long ago
and from today:
Emotion should always be contained
and it is
in these shining beauties
these obelisks and brimming coffins
finally
it is.

The Button Collector

This is common   I'm told
and I open   the box of chocolates
swallow   the paving stone   of milky sugar   and   another
common I'm told.

The man   she said   collects buttons
he has cards of them   each gripping
the rectangle of cardboard with its   discrete metal claw
the loop   where the thread and tether go.

There's a red one   in the shape of a heart
and I open my lips   and shove the cherry in
(this *I*   is not necessarily   me)
I imagine   his back bent   and swooping
the plumage closing   the ragged wings
the beak   taking in   another stone
and now I swallow   a rind encased   in chocolate
ginger   orange peel   coconut cream.

He takes down another   card of buttons   these shaped
like strawberries   buttons made of coral   freckled
with tiny seeds   (these must have cost
a pretty   penny)
I see him close his eyes   and run   his fingers
over the little bumps of bone   the vertebrae
pinned to the card.

So swallow another   (coffee   bitter almond   another
cut of orange peel)
my turn to
take another
and listen   to my empty stomach rattle.

The House

Each post with a stabbing end
the point of silent resolution
pushed into the earth
ensuring the confinement of the house:
brick holly privet fence
enclosing protecting
the arrangement
of bulbs and precious words
words I learned early
rhizomes *tubers* storing food against drought
storing sound twisted
waiting tightfisted under the earth
quince *Jerusalem artichoke* *blackcurrant*
names by which to navigate
the green grass sea *hellebore* *sweet william*
polyanthus *love-in-a-mist*
code words to be passed hand to hand at the gate
but there was no gate
just a space
no unnecessary construction
because we had the silence
to slam into place
across and
against.

In the Greenhouse

My mother   in the greenhouse   looking
at peppers rising   under glass
the rounding sheen   of orange flesh
the waxy skin
magnified
by her attention   she of the cool   assessing eye
judgment suspended   above
every person   every place
judgment   a righteous fiery wheel   turning
fixing the air
above every trespassing object
daring to be special.

My mother looking down
allowed them to be beautiful.

Watching   I turned into my surprise   that something
so humble
could   have pleased her
fiery wheel turning   measuring
inevitable
judging every venture   space   object   human
to be   sensible
or   worthless
so that   afterward
my life has seemed
a single act
of
salvage.

At the Inn

We walk   up the steps
through the heavy doors   authority   stiffening the hinges
into the sanctuary   the nave
the smoke   the hearth smell
crackling
pushing me back   into the fires
we had in the old house:
the yellow curtains   the bubbling wallpaper
William Morris crawling   over the fabric
the blackbird stealing strawberries   dropping them into his hungry beak
pushing me back to Dad   reading
Sherlock Holmes   rounded vowels   Sir Arthur Conan Doyle
flaming
pushing me back   to
smoking world-void   hungry fireplace
the absence.

At the inn now
we step between bronze lions
you touch the mane   as I did   daughter
and the sparks fly.

I guide you past the grandfather clock (don't stop for memories there)
past the magic carpet
past the gray   ambassador cat
you touch the lions again
you come into the pool of the quiet room
where you sit enthroned   daughter
and I see you   leaning   back

into the tawny-threaded seat
staring at the grand terrain   hearing
the tongue-clicking of the clock
ticking the debris   the memories away
leaning into this perfection   the embracing arms   of this old
wooden   chair
the lions   the throne   your melting hair.

How many people   I asked you   have walked here
how many   have sat in your place   in this chair
have felt as warm as you?
You hum
and I step forward   from behind the thieving curtain
this time   I'm the blackbird
I take the strawberry
I gobble it   down my half-starved throat
I crush the juice   smear it
all over my   mother's beautiful red chair
and I smooth   my hands over   and along
feeling the slender
wooden
arms.

Thank you
I won't sit.

Tulips Require Partial Shade

This grief without tears
standing beside the pile of dishes
thinking *Here we are again*
because there are two women
standing at the sink
the one I thought I'd be with a poem turning in her head
words tumbling vying seeking their escape
and the one I am this one is cleaning
forever brushing someone else's teeth
taking care.

At the sink that one composes
a poem about tulips
she takes the words out twangs them like elastic
while this one—she the shadow sister—
this one turns on the tap to sponge another plate
she prepares to fill out the papers
to choose the right music
taking care daughter
to soothe your undeferrable anxiety.

We are tulips the ghostly kind we are
blood-red streaks narrow stripes against the white
slitting the silken tube
the waxy peeling skin.

It says on the packet that we require partial shade
it does not give the bloom time.

No solid speculator would acquire us

we three:
the two   standing   at the sink
and thee
(you will always be *thee* to me   daughter).

After it happened   I numbed
composed my skin
I prepared to hollow out the earth
to take us in.

PART TWO

AWE

Where Does the Rapunzel Go?

The girl six years old playing on the boulder
face crammed to the rock hands gripping the cord
of braided living fiber:
Look, it's like Rapunzel's hair!
It's a vine says her mother.

She is tough the girl rappelling down the rock
swinging climbing restless sparking.

Where does the Rapunzel child go?
Is she ground down by offices errands conveyor belts
to dust
while the list of commodities for sale
diamonds beauty-in-tubes phones guns
waits
harvesting anything that strays?

There Is No Formula for Fox

It is   astonishment   recognition   body-joy
I see a fox   (twice a week   here)   *vulpes   vulpes!*
it is itself   disappearing   into itself   and again   itself   there is no
shading   into anything else   the audacious unrepeatable
and the fox goes down the road   light feet
the tilt of the face
whittle and poise and shock   of red   unnegotiable
and I cannot get there
I cannot know it   through words   cannot drag it slowly through
my understanding
the way I could   a dog   a horse   a lizard
and when I see a fox   I
think of my daughter:
There is no formula for fox.

Love Poem: Daughter

Extortionate and painful   love
the trampoline   jumps and ditches   and returns
she holds up her elbow   to be kissed
jutting out one   then the other   like a winged   bony butterfly
and now let us rock   and now let us dance   and now kiss my elbow
the elbow is the hinge   the turning of the arm.

The occasional pronouncement   spelled out   with a finger   on the keys
painstaking   and always
true
the turn of the head   her head turning   to look back
over her shoulder   the bright darkness of the calculating eye
affection crashing through   her body
tearing off   my hat   hurling it upon the floor   each gesture   a flourishing
a rip-roaring   gesture of   the small-town   theater circuit.

Throws it on the floor   pulls me bodily toward her   and
looking into   my eyes   pupil to pupil
like snaps homing on a coat   willing me   not
to look away
aiming her lips at the middle of my forehead where   my cyclops eye would be
drilling her mouth   into the skin   there   as if to bore   straight
through
to my skulled mind   the looping pandemonium
and then another kiss   and another
storming through   the thinking
her hands   grip
her eyes stay   locked
there is no escape
I would not want it:
Abundance.

Walking on a Keyboard

I remember my daughter's toy   a strip of vinyl   laid
out on the tiled floor
colored keyboard   she could walk upon
each step pressing   launching   sound
each step treading out a note   a charge   a jarring question
speaking   with her toes.

My daughter did not choose it   the music
so I rolled it   hid it   silenced   in the basement   dull and closed
slipped it   under a rug.

Another year
opening the door   pool of shadows   tugging at a single bulb
I stepped across it
exploded   into   the trapped   and crouching   sound
memories   rattling and striking
my convalescent skin
collecting the notes
notes   sent
to myself
from another time   returning me   so that
I climb
awe   struck
into the past

Again.

Planting

I walked out here   head pushed down
panting for air.
looking   into the soft darkness   of the soil   down
into the promise that   will take the roots
placing my hands around the girth   hands spanning   burying
the plant I've neglected   dying in a borrowed pot
rosebush
pushing the root   down   to await the verdict.

Dusk is lowered   eyes adjusting
inhaling tiny points of light:
the fireflies   are out.

Fingers pawed   into the soil
the ancient scent
medieval words come back to me   When Adam delved and Eve span
digging   smelling up the breathing scent
caving back   into myself.

I drop the keys   splay brass fingerbones across the stones
(keys to the house   keys to the car).

Finished: squatting in the darkness   feeling the edges falling
edges dropping
into the fatty velvet dark
where taste   is smell   is touch   is sound
where particles   snug together   and unflint.

Watching the fire seeds   watching
and becoming animal skin   back to the state
where it's impossible to name

the separate obstacles   where there's only
the hissing of surround.

Now the stars come round again
sprinkling lush across the dark
dark   waiting for the fox to shriek.

In the morning   I belt myself in
I prepare to drive back   into the noise   again
back to the state of edges
where every space comes ridged and measured
traffic light   asphalt strip   pavement line
knowing I will be
parceled out of rapture.

Two Figures on the Path

After a bleak distracted day: Beauty
it's rolling us up.

Two small plodding figures on the trail
darkly trodden leaves wintry chill
the sky thinned blue steel floating on light
balanced between lines of sycamores gray-chalk-white
ghost-blanching bark scaling
devoutly catching the cleanest light.

When the light strikes the leaves the path converts
to pure light a flashing arrow
Look! I shout
Stella cannot speak but her words
break out in illuminated moments
burst through her fingers
she turns now touches her fingers to her chest
meaning *Yes, bring it to me.*

I tell myself not to be ashamed to think
in such unpinched words
(I'm porpoising between *euphoric* and *sublime)*
just because it took me so much effort to learn
not to be ashamed of beauty
not to shout when confronted *I'm a grown-up!*
I don't believe in spells.

Walking here with my daughter
I decide to splurge
I leave my mind

a few steps back   propped
against a fence post   waiting to be   retrieved
on an ordinary   cutting   day.

Stella   touches her fingers to her heart again
Look!   I shout   and we walk together
straight
into the fire.

No Wonder

I

I run along the sand   with
my mouth open   hooting
singing it all up   the wonder   digging it out of the wet sand
with my little shovel
the warming questions   the puzzles
scooping them up.

I'm four years old   this is before school
comes to mangle my private soul   before it attacks
making the unimportant   urgent   and cruel
taking everything that used to matter   burying it cold
lies   spreading like gravy   ladle after ladle.

II

I'm in the classroom   I'm nine years old
my sparkling hands   unvoiced   because
I can't read
can't write   (I'm *slow*)
put your pail away   your shovel down
turn back to the long dust
plod
practice tying the laces of your shoes
measure earthworms   and other useful things
sieve off the beauty
because   nothing mysterious   can be allowed
to traitor through.

It's time to
enter the gates   of the school   hang your wonder up
over there   on the peg   beside your coat.

Wonder

She is touching light.

Now she presses *speak*
pressing the bar that converts the letters into sound
(as if it's a matter of persuasion)
it's all there torching
through the illuminated screen.

Sometimes when she types I laugh
(pure wonder)
then it's her turn the swimming giggle the rollicking river-squiggle
happiness
both of us laughing because the words are
free.

It's back:
my famished wonder booming
all the shining questions puzzles
scars delirious inconsistencies
I'm shoveling them up shaking the light
across the rediscovered land.

Her fingers move type another word
press the bar to speak:
the words are spelling
OUT O-U-T.

My daughter's here
I'm back
I'm running along the sand hooting
singing it up.

A Child

She was podded in me before
they slit the skin fabric
with a knife
disbursing a single rolled-up seed.

My eyes half opened: I saw her
held above the bloodline of my stomach
her eggshell self-containment rendered
by a finical Dutch painter.

In my mind I saw
the painter's hand
conjuring a lemon
the line of umbilical skin
pith-lined dimpled peel curving
over the edge of the doctor's blue-scrubbed arms—
which had become
the artist's painted table—
and my eyes closed
on the jaundiced spiral unwinding golden
back to the wound.

Later I watched her shift on the hospital bed beside me
each time the sheets stirred painting a new spirit:
an ermine her sleek thin face
sharp eyes alert to everything
and ready to bolt.

I watched   the sheets   twist
vibrating in their whiteness
around   their newfound center
I felt it then: wonder
with a little cut of terror.

The Mouse and the Hawk

I'm a mouse racing beneath
the hawk's almighty gaze
eyes rippling my fur invisible tingling caress.

Getting smaller smaller
I'm a running flashing light
I'm a legged torch burning a trajectory of fear
across the choppy ground
the grass blades of the forest
my skin's thinning my fur's sliding off lifting
in a neat evacuated pocket
I'm prey rising into the uncanny perforated sky.

I wake up gasping running my hands
over the blankets striping them with fear
waiting for the next dream to arrive
a belittling scooping terror
each terror dropped at an equal distance
parcels streaming faster than my arms can take them
Stop thinking I tell myself *don't think … just count*
and I'm off running again …
the grass disappears drops flat in a single breath
against the soil I'm
exposed
the hawk beams down
prepares to dive
to spear me in its flawless beak now
I'm in the murder.

I pray: *Turn me around*
give me the talons
make me the predator
let me wreak small murder
and surprise another animal
in its cowering blood.

Hurt

In honor of the sculpture The Penitent Magdalene *by Donatello, circa 1440*

Sitting in a plastic chair
in a room stuffed with bodies   students   their indifference
filling the room like static
sitting in the dark
(this was long ago   when slides came in carousels
when we watched each image replace the last   in a beam of light
clearing the way   occasionally
for an absolute god   of revelation)
the slide came on
I didn't know who she was
Human   I thought
or I might have thought   *Hurt*
Human   *Throat*
there was nothing between me and the body
boring through the light
hunger eyes   clawed out of wood
hair   the only mercy   clothing you
but I did not know this then
I saw gouts of thickened blood   I saw an animal
in a wild hide
I saw blood becoming tears   flowing
from an open wound
there was no art   no intermediary
only pain   chopped and sliced
pitched out of the light at me
Donatello   said the teacher's voice
Magdelene:
you hit me like an arrow
in the neck.

Elijah

I

Not that I needed a prophet
not that I wheeled around   following   the spins of faith
I was catlike   in my cabin   biding
my time   insensibly   happy
a cabin   next to a henhouse   abandoned
full   of   filthy straw   old tin pails
enough room for a single   lop-winged hen.

I found water running
in the stream beside
the glass walls   of the cabin
violets in a meadow   spread
a blanket waiting
for a pre-Raphaelite head
in the fall   the cabin was used   to hold the carcasses of deer
they dragged them in   to count
their bloody   broken   heads.

No electricity   everything had to be taken cold
I lived on bread and licorice
feeding the stove   my warm belly   poking through the ash
winging into solitude   those first   endless   rainy days.

The rain stopped   the snakes came out
baking their scales   on the gravel path.

I dragged my easel   down the road
with each step   I raised my foot   waiting   to see
if the basking shadow moved
counting   counting twelve

copperheads
twelve   indolent princesses
coiled   waiting.

In the cabin   on the edge of the mattress   I dropped
my head between my knees:
shoulders slumping   legs thinning
my cicada-body   muttering and churring
fear   exploding   inside my insect skull.

II

The door opened:
the cat   stepped in   half-grown
striped tail   orange fur
an unnecessarily beautiful creature
watching me   from across the room.

The air's wheezing   zagging   the cat's claws lashing   striking
the cat and the snake   are fighting
(small snake   mere start of a cat)
it's impossible   this vision
too strenuous   too quick
I watch   feeling my incompetence
I'm not the right witness   for this struggle.
The cat's claws   knife down—
they must break the streaming creature
stop the incoherence
the looping muscle   that is always   rushing into
the afterimage   of itself.

The cat killed the snake (is this a children's book?)
and I pitched the carcass   in the stream
watched it turn back   into a stick
emptied   unglossed   carried on the current
out of my Eden.

I called the cat *Elijah*
I invited him in.

A Demonstration

Rottweilers two slow black boulders foggily curious
I'm afraid they will scoop him up eat him like jam:
the kitten lying on the stoop Elijah
a tiny jar of light.

Elijah sees them stares them down
bursts into his Greater Beast
fearless an animal starting gun:
Take this, you fiends! POW! BAM! SPLAT!
he's spitting his legs are stiff his back is arched
he's an exaggerated creature
drawn by someone who can barely hold a pencil
stiff legs on springs
ludicrous wind-up fur.

The dogs fade to whimper.

Elijah steeples and explodes
the dogs go up in smoke.

I put a saucer down and
watch the kitten lap a little milk
into the delicate pink grotto of his mouth.

Who needs a self-help book
when you've witnessed such a demonstration?

Life Jacket

Mine   it is pure   this memory   I sink down into it
yet it is hard to   get the difficulties clear   to strike them   cleanly
match after match
I remember   the suck and breath   of the water advancing and receding
the hairy-rinded flesh   clinging to the stony walls.

I remember painting in the cave
sitting inside   the scooped-out rock
sitting on a stone   ledge   the water lapping
over my booted feet   the crinkling light.

I remember painting in a cave
the chilly wetness spreading   through my thighs
my knees flaring outwards
crooking sharply   into flaking walls
a canvas balanced   on my knees
a life jacket   with brushes stuck
through the belt
pulling   each one   out of my soft armor
my inflatable skin
this is the closest I can come   to swallowing the painting
I must change   into a different creature   not relying
on names   or words   that I throw over the landscape
using them   like nets   to haul the truth home   always restless
to stand up   with an explanation   I need to become   invertebrate
an octopus perhaps   trailing my delighted limbs   across
these trenches filled   with easy   spilling pigment.

PART THREE

THE SMALL DOMESTICS

Little Gratitudes

For Siri France

Sailing   into the   Little Gratitudes again:
Ann Sather's by the "L"   the Belmont stop.

We could only afford to go there
when the money pooled   between our hands
a few dollars ushering in
doughy slabs   ample   crusted with sugar
coiled in cinnamon and butter.

Piranesi's   endless grimy intersecting columns   alleys   smells
parcels of rickety land
it's a city of the mind   Chicago
so in my mind   the memory of   waitresses   moving   in white costumes
stenciled with nostalgia   moving
through the solicitous fog   of the restaurant   a ship paddling through cloud
through snow falling   falling slowly   through the dappled evening
snow   was never weather for us   it was a rumor   a spell
proving   we had landed somewhere else
in the hospitable *Here*   where the waitresses smiled   even
when   we ordered another coffee   and another
because we could not believe   that
refills   were free   in this country
(I know now that they are not   and some cups will always
be left empty).

I can't give you up
waitresses   women   in stamped aprons   moving
in my memory   you've become
Mothers with platters   bringing food

before we close the door
and walk back into the freeze
Mothers bent   upon filling our spindly legs   with warmth
which is something
I’ve come across
in fiction.

At the Salon

His soft echo   breathes   half a beat behind
a mirror   image in the air-water
so natural   it's like a second hip moving   in the dance
(I don't know any of these songs   and if I did
I wouldn't be able to keep   a single note).

The blade nips in   the hair drops
onto the floor   becoming   immediately alien
this severed human part   a straight lock
mingling with the others on the floor
black   blond   brown   gray   red
this is the closest we will come   these locks
of people I will never meet   except through
our indifferent   interlocking hair.

The hair is used as compost   the stylist tells me
so my hair   and hers   and his   and theirs
will soften   will break down   will collapse
fall into the melting vegetable ocean
and   I think   as I watch another lock fall   onto the floor
that a bird might pick it up
before the hair has lost   the distinction of its shape
and the bird will weave it   into the architecture
of her nest   threading
silky   coarse   dry   and   lush
aged   hollowed   split
so we will tremble in the breeze together
become a cupholder for song.

In this vision   the bird is weaving   moss   bark   lint   human
there's a hair's-breadth division   between my cut self

an inch of snakeskin   and
a plastic ribbon …
and the hair of the woman   in the chair
next to mine   is falling …
now   we're fanning out across the floor
now   we're swept and broomed across the tiles
through the beat of the song
the words of the song
comes the stylist's voice   half a beat behind
circling   sweetening   the room
so that
the padded chairs   bottles and vials   mirrored
in the glass behind us—
an apothecary's shelf of colored syrup—
glow   are wrapped and shimmered
in swimming rills of sound   and
through the window   on the sill
I see
a scruffy sun-washed sparrow
looking in.

Butter and Milk and Sugar

Bales of hay   wrapped in white plastic
lined   like a wall of marshmallows   in front
of a deep-red barn
Thank you   I think   as I drive past   as if
they had been arranged
for me.

Everything combines to make this day:
the hospitable rain   the music coming from the radio
trumpets   trombones with their brassy jaunt.

I'm as happy   as a child   leaning
over the big pan   on the stove
driving my wooden spoon along the bottom
watching the butter and milk and sugar   bubble
knowing that when they part
letting me see a clean path of metal
it will be ready:
fudge
all the sugar   I can eat.

Driving past   a dozen graves
I see Moses-Abigail   Jonathan   Jeremiah-Zillah
as we pass   she blurs═
Zill≡lah════
pulled into the warp of the trombone
her name rounding   disappearing into
its   brave   magenta sound.

The Only Unextraordinary Things

The samplers in the parsonage at Howarth
watch me   from behind the glass
at first glance   they're the only unextraordinary things.

I see the sweat gather in your needles
slicking the thin spoke of the metal
piercing   rising   ducking   striking
the laborious censored work
of stitching to order
pricking your scrupulous fingers.

The long eye   the blunt   slow point of the needle
sowing determination   *chain* stitch   *seed* stitch   *queen*
now you can proceed to *fly*   Charlotte   and   at last to *running*
(which in a sampler is not permitted)
drawing sweat in and out of the canvas
pulling it through
to thread the gaps with color
because   the spaces in the linen
are the only space you've got.

The fast nib   the point of the pen   playing
quick unrepeatable
making Rochester
Bertha
Jane
because   *There was no possibility of taking a walk that day.*

At This Distance Safely Brilliant

My mother told me   that Emily taught herself German
while she kneaded the bread   the book propped up on the table.
This frightened me
the girl who   at ten   could not read or write
what was I bound for?

Charlotte was obedient   Mum thought
and   at this distance   safely brilliant
or was this   what my mother   told herself   as she
stooped over the dough
which she had made from scratch
to keep her hands busy
kneading   pummeling   to unlearn   her own
acquired language
which was bare   knuckled
silence.

Thank You for Your Patience

The pearls come in seeds   they can be cultivated
or baroque   and there are the pirate kind
which do not exist individually   but by the lungful
in chests below the sea
rising like bubbles through our dreams.

Pearls   the unlicensed thoughts
of a child   unable to understand the lesson
when numbers   letters
fly by   matted   dark   relentlessly significant.

When you're an adult staring at the autocratic page
your pen poised to knock out every nonsense-box
on the form
when you're on hold   swinging from the phone tree   waiting
waiting   *Thank you for your patience…*
these pearls   become the relics from a grander life
you might have lived
you might have stepped   slim-footed down the stairs
idling in light-splashed satin.

Might   but here you are   waiting
(Your call will be answered in the order
it was received)
waiting
trying to hold on to   your single strand
of   cultivated
pearls.

Longing

Vermeer's girl   her pearl earring
beckoning   suspended like a radiant fingertip   swinging
ready to place itself   between your lips.

And   for others   a string of pearls polished
them off   made them clean
and ready to unwrap.

I wanted seed pearls   trapped   and strung
like beads of lustrous sweat   around my throat
I'd bring them back   for women
for men
for any child   who has ever wanted
to make   their longing   to be seen
solid
to hang it shining
round their neck.

Feasts

Pearls
shot in volleys   at the tablecloth
at the feast   landing in bumpy crusts across
the quilted gowns   of plump-fingered women
bending to lift their goblets of painted wine
women in gowns shaped like bells   like padded rusty swans
sewn with Veronese's pearls.

The Last Meal

For Selma Putterman, 1930–2008

The last meal we ate   together:
I see
Selma   slicing strawberry pie
choosing the most succulent parts
dropping them onto Stella's plate   murmuring words
not words that order   or describe
words as binding warmth   words as swaddling cloth
face of my heart   she said to Stella   *face of my heart*
scent of strawberries   juice of strawberries   mixing with the words
the partiality of memory   melting in the mouth   recombining
two faces   each intent upon the other
two faces
above
the tines of a single fork
two faces waiting
to be hatched again
into a new wonder
and a different song.

PART FOUR

ANXIETIES

On the Clock

I was stopped
in traffic   at the light
when I saw her
she walked   into the alley
streaked through heckling twilight
slumped herself
into the chair   a swivel chair   black legs complicated
bent and gripping like a spider
she collapsed herself into it   the waitress
dropped like a cratering sack   deadheading herself   a casualty
lighting a cigarette   a woman in a white top   black skirt
revolving in her seat   fingers holding the cigarette   her head
tilted back
the fire-tip spinning
the radium-coated hand   of a speeding clock
then   she handed herself back
passed through the door
to the engine room
serving food   serving time   money-ticking.

And I put the car in gear
I prepared to drive away   and
forget her.

Hush

Inspired by Caspar David Friedrich's Woman at a Window*, 1822*

Where quietness runs   like a wire   through her body
wire   holding her taut   focusing the beam
the thin and narrow   of her life
holding back   the roar
the voice that stains   the muslin   of her dress   as she stands
mouthing words   at the open   of the window
feeling the song   gather   and warm   in her throat
her ankles waiting   like   a pot   boiling
beneath the hem   the simmer   of her dress:
Hush.

Small Word

I catch it at the end of her letter:
love me
(is it *love me*?   or   *love, me*?   what does a comma do?)
me   a grain   dropped in the darkness   a light in the mud
turning   considering revival.

I know from that syllable   peeled   exposed   in its smallness
on the page: *me*
dropped like Goya's tiny painted dog   dark-snouted face   edging
from the pit   staring into eons of illuminated dust
I know   that she does not dare   to write her name
she's reduced it   to a stump of self
to a snail's withdrawing foot:
me.

I know   it's been a   crushing day
a pitcher filled with silence   flung   to extinguish
dancing
larking around
and every other sort of   humble nonsense.

Shatterproof

I

I'm packing my old   drawing things   away
coming across the ruler
shatterproof it says
who is?   who isn't faintly chipped?
who isn't   in need of constantly
supporting drifts of sugar?

Shatterproof   it cannot be broken   but it
can be fractured   like a window   shield
the glass dividing into stranded cells
(the effect is known as   *crazed).*

I pick up the ruler   hold it in my palm
trying to transfer the strength   or perhaps the memory
putting the weight of it   back in my hand   of being young
and knowing that
when I lifted my hand   for another charcoal slash   a slam
of the black line down
a little of the dust spluttering ... when
my wrist ripped across the white of the page
getting the line of the chin   down
in a single swipe
bending from the hip feeling power pushing through   preparing to bring
my hand round again ...
knowing   that I'd need just
just two seconds   and round again   no hesitation
drawing the spin of the pelvis   the jut of the knee—
it was all so fast   the living of keen
and I was the commander.

Dynamic poses they called them I could study the model
for a few beats then I knew how to
pull it off
…and round again dragging the stick of charcoal rolling it over
flicking it through the bone of the shoulder
building up the human.

I wouldn't make it palatable
or proficient I'd make it old-fashioned beautiful
wild left over
bristling like a field of stubble
introverted layers glittering half-cut
I'd make it glinting-hard streaked broken shafts of corn
because when I drew
I knew I was exempt
I was shatter proof.

II

Eraser pencil sharpener I'm jamming them back in
the tools the debris of that other life
all the threads I can't hold on to the tensile strength I thought I'd be
the female spider slinging lines of silk from every post
waiting to catch
the model or the lover racing through.

The charcoal crumbles as I
shove it back into the case and prepare
to zipper up.

H Is Drawing

I

H is drawing   I stand at her shoulder   watch the pencil gripped
in her forcing hand   driving the lead
up the steep of the exercise
I walk away   though   I want to touch her shoulder   wish her sweet
release   one of those   lovely forgotten phrases   from
an Elizabethan poem   a phrase to offer succor   (Raleigh says:
Give me my scallop shell of quiet,
my staff of faith to walk upon).

Her lips are tight   the line of the lead   creeps out of her
like a silenced tongue
I pass between the other students   glance at their mild work
walk past H again   her face intent as a nesting oven
What is she drawing?
She is drawing an eraser   plunked down in front of her
she's scrubbing   out the lines   again and again
she's squeezed inside the echo.

The point of the pencil pushes   against the grain
the eraser makes itself   through labor
(H is pains taking)
the eraser has turned into a plinth
it's a monumental stone.

II

In the dream   the eraser   appears in front of me
now there are ten   now twenty
rising   settling
building themselves into a wall   the wall grows
the eraser-blocks   have made a house

three pigs are dropped
into the scene   like dice
from the cupping hand above
and   here comes the wolf   her eyes staring
though the sleep-light   she is
hunger   looking back at me
her claw   is poised above the roof   ready for the   tearing
her nails flex   extend   they lengthen into pencils
stabbing   sinking their points   into the flesh
of the eraser-house
pinning the house to the table   so that it will   never move
so that H will always be sitting   in her chair   drawing
taking pain
so that   she will go on pushing the pencil   go on erasing   grinding
through the lines   leaving little rags of skin behind.

The quotation is from "The Passionate Man's Pilgrimage" by Sir Walter Raleigh, 1618.

PART FIVE

THE SLEEPLESS EYE

Trapped

I

The boy stopped young over his boots
the terrible start of it
a punch that cleared the morning light
beauty caught and cracked
red fur
eyes stretched in pain if you took pain—if you could touch pain if
it became a palpable thing and you bowled it like a weighted ball
toward the brain I saw it hit home crash
into the animal skull.

The summer I was nine
tramping with the boy across
the acres of his farm walking side by side
rubber boots shoving their way like blunt black muzzles through
the thick grass we were looking for traps
the poachers set them in the flat framed fields
I pictured rabbits tufts of silky fur waiting (we would release them).

Fox I thought it was alive
I can see its raging eyes (the eyes are gas-flame blue
a shock of white tearing twisting through)
I reached out to touch the fur found a noose I hadn't seen
a snag of wire death circling
tightening around its throat.

I thought it was alive
thought I could see that deranging pain still hot
in its flickering eye
I reached out touched its fur
trying to catch it and return it to the moment
before its soul pressed through.

II

For years I didn't think about it
then in 2020 when disease was spreading
fixing us snaring us so that I felt as if I could chew my own feet
I was walking along the path beside the creek I saw the sun
roaring through the fall trees
a sugar maple taking fire
red-orange leaves
red pelt jumping through
and it came back to me that stricken captive face
details came back I had forgotten
the matted fur around its throat
slippery dark
fingered into points and styled with blood.

That year the plague year the year of loneliness
I dreamt that face through the night
the cub again forty nights perhaps
in that forsaken year
forty twistings and re-livings
my own thoughts noosed anxiety straining at my throat
starting startling again
I see its eyes
its outraged face
its fear
an education in cruelty.

And they trundled out the bodies wheeling across the screen
again and again until I turned away
until I saw the creature's face again the slaughtered beauty.

And so   that year   we turned against each other
and I look back
at our cruelty
unmasked.

Witch

The year   when death came axing through the land
when each tall life   was felled
and wrapped
and sparks of missed love jumped   the tracks.

Old words reliving   *plague*   *pestilence*   the dreaded random
that we try to   remake into a marketable legend
because arbitrary pain   becomes indecent.

The year I kept making   the same cup of coffee
with worshipful diligence
as if   through this attention
I could renew   remake the day   begin again
force the ravenous spite   of death
to reconsider.

Let me measure out the grounds more carefully
(let me use a different measure)
this time   I'll smooth the grounds   with the side of my hand
this time   I'll use an unbleached filter
this time…

Each time I start again   to make a different cup
hoping to watch the steam rise
against the background   of a different kitchen
a room dropped down   in a safe land.

One day   I start to brew
and catch myself   I'm standing at the sink
watching a deer   nudge the hoard of grass   below the window
watching my reflection   I notice

I've become a witch
there in the glass   is a woman bent
upon brewing the perfect potion
hoping that   by the faintest grass blade   of adjusted balance
she can cheat   the tally
she can protect   her own
send grief to someone else's door.

Tasting the latest brew   I shake my head:
unsatisfactory
I wait while the world outside   remains
fathomlessly   agnostically cruel
then I measure out the grounds again
and climb the stairs   to check
on my twin compass points   of love.

A Single Sleepless Eye

Coming back from the contamination   of the store
moving round the kitchen   I imagine that
each time   my finger lands upon a surface
the counter   the sink   the doorknob
my touch leaves a ghosting incriminating glow
fingerprints gathering   on the table   the spoon   the faucet
in livid overlapping frills
phosphorescing   turning the arms of the chair
into gulping innuendo
I sit down   rest my hands securely
on the spectral branches.

I close my eyes   and tell myself   not to run
through the house crying   "The sky is falling in!"
I tell myself   *Have no fear*   *Little Chicken.*

I pull the blanket up   to my daughter's chin
hoping that   at night   she can escape the attention
of the year that has become
a single sleepless eye.

The Drummer

Staring at the deer again   I try to believe   that at this moment
in New York   people are banging saucepans and skillets
shaking their arms   with firecrackers taped to their wrists
the din   exploding from balconies and windows
(I picture ballerinas   cleaners firefighters   stockbrokers and teachers)
I picture a percussionist   drumming   working the pedal with her foot
leaning in   with her crowding happy shoulders
(she can rumpus every space with sound now
there's no need   to think about the neighbors).

At my window   the deer is joined by another
and over the days   I watch the grain disappear   from the feeder
I listen on the radio   to the surprise of those
who are not used to isolation.

Outside her room   New Yorkers
pound   and shout   as their power drains away
It's   the sound of solidarity   says the voice on the radio
but it hits the air   like a rattling metal scream
steel fists   smashing on the door
forty floors up   banging to be let out
wondering what fresh shock   will be delivered
from this confinement
this labor   forty floors up.

Here   looking at the deer   in the green yard
New York is fictional
while on the radio   a voice commands us to be *mindful*
and I picture   people moving soundlessly from room to room
carrying their calm and shapely brains   on trays.

The voice on the radio recites the rosary of common truth
the words   this time   has gathered:
healing closure coping mechanisms sourdough grief
looking out of the window at another streamlined deer
oblivious   whole   trim in every shellacked hoof
while   on the radio   the woman clicks through the sacred words again:
healing digital divide virtual pod Zoom Zoom.
And before we know
it will be gone
the nerve of this   the affront   of this year
it will have become *that* year
the past
a memory   vanishing like   rain
down the gutter.

While in New York   the girl drums
and learns to wear her tee-shirt like a surplice.

Each Small Castle Window

Words held   scared   inside our separate houses
fear   lined and bottled   on the windowsills…
I'm walking at dusk   past the trapping houses
trying to decode the secrets of their fronts   the clue   of light
that burns in each small castle window…
walking down the emptied Covid streets
between the silent voices
when
a car whooshes by   shooting through the window
the cannon of an ecstatic nosy head
a loopy-woolly-walrus-dog   grinning   streaming wild hair
a master   of the pantomime-joy-thesaurus
shedding wonder   love
cruising it through the brittle air.

This poem is for dogs
with nostrils as delicate as ferns
who've stormed
the quiet line of my despair.

Bears

For Carol Stewart, the mudlarker in question
(Mudlarkers comb the mud of tidal rivers searching for lost historical objects.)

I

Sugar molds!   I shout   *Mudlarking!*
I'm not sure why   this fills me with delight
(this is during Covid   the first winter
frozen light   cutting through the glass   covering
the floor   with its dead-white chill   looking down
at my slow-filled hands   feeling snow melt   on my thin neck).

My friend fished them out of the Thames   darting the beak of her hand
winkling for grubs of silver and gold   in the congenial slime
What is a sugar mold?   I ask
It's made of copper   it's a cone   they used to pour sugar in them—
look it up
on the internet   I find an image   a dented brown cone   it looks like
an animal snout   a bear's nose
(I watch a clip of bears   fattening for winter).

Sugar cones   why   I ask her
haven't I come across them in fairy tales?
Isn't a sugar cone as worthy as a spindle   or a thorn?

I listen   with my daughter   to a book about the Arctic
we sit   on the edge   of the bed
I listen to her heavy breath   I wonder
if we have enough fat   to survive   the cold time
the time for eating and preserving
I tell myself to hold   the sugar cone
until it melts in my hands.

II

I am hungry
there's a pastry   I remember   called a *bear claw*
it's made with almonds and sugar
and there's another *cache museau*   or   in English
hide-the-muzzle.

I press the arrow   to hear the next chapter
we go on listening   in silence
to the voice   only the voice   and the sound
of my amazement   flying
in the sort of gratitude   that cooks in the stomach
like silk from a spider   and I listen as the voice tightens
the enchantment
and I think of bears in their dark snug
and I know now   that   she understands   every word.

This is the first time we've   listened to a book   together
since Stella learned to speak   again
since she   typed herself back   into her voice
her fingers on the tablet   on the keyboard.

She was content   we listened   for hours that day
all the way through   in peace
tunneled   in the cave of her breath.

Climb out of the upstairs den   meet the spring
buds sprout   tiny green claws—
Clear the way
We're coming!

ACKNOWLEDGMENTS

Thank you to Sarah Bauhan, Henry James, and Joal Hetherington at Bauhan Publishing for their exceptional generosity in considering every detail of this book.

Thank you, Victor, for your love and solidarity, even in the most difficult times.

Thank you, Stella, my intense, luminous daughter. Your extraordinary character has opened up a new world to me.

Thank you, Richard Smith, author of the unforgettable collection, *Not a Soul but Us,* for reading this manuscript with such understanding and wisdom.

I started to write these poems in the autumn, in the land of foxes. Sometimes, I saw foxes several times a week; every encounter with a fox is a gasp of wonder. I continued to work on the manuscript through a move and a long winter. Then, in the spring, I began to see bears: six magnificent bears. Thank you.

PRAISE FOR *RECEIPT FOR LOST WORDS*

Receipt for Lost Words is a mother's attempt to understand a world in which her child does not, cannot speak. It's an accounting that Catherine Arnold renders in breathtakingly moving, spaced-apart phrases, little gasps of insight into a parent's heartbreak, bafflement, and isolation: "Nature now   is what I see   through glass." And, if we hold our breath through desperate parental denial and efforts to "word the silence," we release it when Stella—the one who cannot speak—makes her presence known: "the strong   unhurried length   of me / I am Stella." The spare, sensual language of Stella's point of view stuns—as in this description of her father: "a big   thirsty shape / the hum of him." What emerges is a new sense of the world, a magical and fairy-tale shift in which ". . . everything / that seemed to matter   before / has been forgotten." Catherine Arnold has accomplished nothing less than the embodiment, in words, of wordlessness. A moving receipt for what has been lost.

—**REBECCA KAISER GIBSON**, judge of the May Sarton New Hampshire Poetry Prize and author of *Girl as Birch* and *Opinel*

In *Receipt for Lost Words*, Catherine Arnold writes, "My daughter possessed it once / (speech) / and then she lost   it / how will it be   for us   to dwell in a wordless land?" In this probing debut collection, the speaker interrogates the power and limits of language in a quest to understand her daughter's experience of the world. The result is a wonder of cerebral lyricism, an essayist's sustained attention paired with a poet's image-centered consciousness. Beyond "all the pinecone words / the kindling   of manageable thoughts," this book blazes its hard, human fire. This is riveting work—hard, beautiful, necessary work.

—**JULIE MARIE WADE**, author of *Skirted* and *Just an Ordinary Woman Breathing*

Catherine Arnold's debut collection, *Receipt for Lost Words*, plunges readers into a world of uncomfortable, deeply necessary truth-telling. With each poem, she invites us into a world of authenticity and awe, unearthing what's sacred in the casual miracles that other parents take for granted. Through compelling metaphor and painstaking detail, she conjures magical worlds in these pages. With beautiful simplicity and keen observation of what is seen and unseen, Arnold illustrates the fierce loyalty and elemental depth of a mother's love. These are poems that will stay with you because they take on poetry's most vital work: to say what will not—or cannot—be said. A stunning debut.

—**AMY TUDOR**, author of *A Book of Birds* and *Studies in Extinction*